Thomas Allan Croal

Scottish Loch Scenery

Thomas Allan Croal

Scottish Loch Scenery

ISBN/EAN: 9783337243432

Printed in Europe, USA, Canada, Australia, Japan

Cover: Foto ©Thomas Meinert / pixelio.de

More available books at **www.hansebooks.com**

SCOTTISH

LOCH SCENERY.

LONDON:
JOHN WALKER

SCOTTISH

LOCH SCENERY.

ILLUSTRATED IN

A SERIES OF COLOURED PLATES

FROM DRAWINGS BY

A. F. LYDON.

WITH DESCRIPTIVE NOTES BY THOMAS A. CROAL.

LONDON:

JOHN WALKER AND CO.

1882.

CONTENTS.

SCOTTISH LOCH SCENERY.

LOCHMABEN.

THE visitor to Scotland, entering from the south, has not far
to travel before he reaches one of the loveliest lowland scenes
the country possesses. The very ancient burgh of Lochmaben lies
on a branch line a little distance from Lockerbie junction, and,
apart from its picturesque surroundings, the old place presents
attractions of its own. It dates from very early times, and its
burghers are known, even to this day, as 'the king's kindly tenants,'
many of the retainers of Robert the Bruce, to whom and whose
ancestors the castle belonged, having obtained rights of property in
one or other of the 'four towns of Lochmaben,' under a tenancy
direct from the Crown, hence forming virtually a proprietary interest.

In Burns's *Five Carlines*, the burgh is called 'Marjory o' the mony
lochs,' from the numerous sheets of water around, of which our
view shows the largest and finest. This is known as the Castle
Loch, and covers about two hundred acres   Although not surrounded by the high mountains and bolder scenery found further north
in Scotland, this loch presents a scene of great beauty, having fine
verdant hills surrounding it, and being itself clothed on every shore
with beautiful woodland scenery.

B

The ruined castle shown in the view occupies a prominent
position upon a heart-shaped peninsula. The visitor will find little
but bare and massive walls to tell him of the extent of this fortress,
once covering sixteen acres in extent, and forming the chief stronghold in the south-west of Scotland. For many years after the castle
fell into ruin it is said the king's tenants used it as a quarry for
building stones, and Chambers, in his *Picture of Scotland*, speaks of
one honest burgher who then 'warmed his toes beside a pair of
fine jambs procured in Bruce's castle.' From the appearance of the
ground, it is evident the neck of the peninsula could be put under
water for defensive purposes, having both an outer and an inner
defence of this kind, besides one or more intermediate fosses that
speak of the same use. The present is not believed to be the
original castle built by the Lords of Annandale, but a subsequent
erection of the thirteenth century. The days of warlike lords and
border forays are over for the Castle of Lochmaben, and now it is
to be regarded merely as a splendid addition to the picturesque
attractions of this very charming district. Boats may be hired for
a row or sail over the placid bosom of the loch, and on a fine
autumn evening no more delightful pleasure could be got.

Besides its other attractions, Lochmaben presents a peculiar fact
in natural history, for in its waters are found—in addition to other
fish—the vendace, a species of fish found in no other loch. It is
popularly but erroneously called a fresh-water herring, for it belongs
to the family of *coregonus*, one of the salmonidæ. This rare fish
takes no lure, and thus can only be netted, and the fishing for it
in the Castle Loch is limited to one day in the year, in July, when
the vendace club meet, fish, and dine. The Mill Loch, another
and lesser of those surrounding the burgh, also contains vendace,
which are fished for one day in August. The Castle Loch measures
a mile long by three quarters broad, the Mill Loch is half a mile
by quarter of a mile, and the other waters are the Kirk-Loch,
Hightae Loch, &c.

LOCII DOON.

A LTHOUGH intimately associated with those scenes to which Burns so plaintively puts the question

> 'Ye banks and braes o' bonnie Doon
> How can ye bloom sae fresh and fair?'

and although it 'pours a' its floods' under that ancient brig where Tam O' Shanter had such a narrow escape, Loch Doon is far from the immediate land of Burns, lying remote in a wild and solitary mountain region. The loch is, however, within four miles of Dalmellington station, and as there is excellent fishing, coaches frequently carry the disciples of Walton, as well as searchers after the picturesque, to this quiet, outlying place. Loch Doon is eight miles in length, and irregular in form, the lower limb of the Loch, from which the river Doon issues, lying to the right as shown in our view. The hills on the south are in the Stewartry of Kirkcudbright, and the loch, forming, over its whole length, the boundary between that county and Ayrshire, is surrounded with pastoral mountains.

At the head of the loch, at its southern end, lies an island on which the remains of an ancient castle are seen. This building, the main feature of which is an octagonal peel or tower formed of large square stones, is only vaguely traceable in history, and at one time belonged to Edward Bruce, brother of Robert the Bruce. Rather more than half a century ago, several canoes were found in the loch near this island, each boat formed from the stem of a single oak tree, the trunk being hollowed out, and the ends finished off in form like a fishing-coble. Common repute gives to such boats an antiquity of eight or nine centuries, but no absolute date can be assigned to them. They belong to what has been called by an eminent Scottish archæologist, non-historic man. Whether they are also pre-historic may be matter of dispute.

The river Doon, for a portion of its course immediately after leaving the loch, presents some very remarkable features. The gully through which it flows gives the appearance of high cliffs rent asunder by some fierce cataclysm to give passage to its waters. The walk along this ravine is singularly striking, the rocks seeming at every turn to close in so as to bar further progress, and when the river is full after a wet season the spectacle is not without elements of terror. All around, the region abounds with lochs, Loch Doon being the largest. Excepting as regards the branch line of railway leading to Dalmellington, the entire district lies apart and silent, a region of hills, occasionally, as in Merrick (2704 feet) and Cairnsmore of Carsphairn (2612 feet), rising to the dignity of mountains, and wholly given up to pastoral uses, except where the iron works around Dalmellington suggest that this upward district touches the border of that mineral wealth which exists so abundantly a little further north.

THE GREY MARE'S TAIL.

WHILE this is not the highest waterfall in Scotland—for the inaccessible Falls of Glomak far exceed all others—the Grey Mare's Tail ranks as one of the most striking. We find amongst the hills at the north-west corner of Annandale, the waters of 'dark Loch Skene,' which find no outlet save over this breakneck descent. Far down in the vale below lies the watering-place of Moffat, famous for its sulphureous springs, clear, cool, and medicinal. Coaches leave this town daily during the season to reach the other side of the hills, and ten miles distant from Moffat this splendid natural phenomenon is seen. The coach, in the slow ascent to the higher level, gives the visitor ample time to find, on foot, the best vantage points from which to see the fall.

When the stream is small, the 'tail' falls off to thin threads of spray, dashed into films of prismatic beauty as they rush from rock to rock. But in spate, the effect comes out in all its grandeur,

'White as the snowy charger's tail.'

and the appropriateness of the name bestowed on the waterfall evidences itself. The entire fall is above two hundred feet at one leap, over a dark rugged precipice, closed in on every side with sharp rocks, and suggesting to the mind ideas of much terror and sublimity. Attempts have been made to scale the face of the fall, occasionally with fatal results, and the imagination can create, even if the eyes cannot see, the fluttering of morsels of clothing that are pointed out by the guide as horrible memorials of such foolhardy attempts. In this wild region were enacted some of the terrible scenes of the Covenanters' persecution. Away in those grim solitudes, 'hunted like a partridge upon the mountains,' the dauntless upholder of the right of private judgment would betake himself, associating with others of like determination. On the 'Watch Hill' opposite Birkhill, the persecuted people set sentinels to signal the approach of Claverhouse or his men, while away in a cave, near a wild waterfall called Dobb's Linn, they held their proscribed services, and here on one occasion the 'bloody Clavers' shot four men, whose graves were marked in Ettrick kirkyard not many years ago. The wild desolation of this scene befits the dark and terrible incidents of which, at this period, it was the scene. The farmhouse of Bodsbeck lies on the road between Moffat and the waterfall, and has been rendered famous in literature through James Hogg, the 'Ettrick Shepherd's' story of the *Brownie of Bodsbeck*, a tale dealing with incidents of the persecution of the Covenanters.

From Moffat can be reached in a different direction some notable hills and ravines, amongst which may be named Hartfell, and Queensberry Hill, from the summit of both of which magnificent panoramas of scenery are opened to view. A remarkable scene is that of the Earl of Annandale's Beef Tub, otherwise called 'The Devil's Beef Tub,' a vast semicircle of precipitous rock, down in the bosom of which many beeves, perhaps driven from other mens' lands, could be hidden away.

ST. MARY'S LOCH.

THERE is no native of Scotland who does not wax poetical when St. Mary's Loch is named. Round it and the district of which it is the crown and glory there centres more of legend, ballad, poem and sentiment than is to be found anywhere else, and in good sooth it is only necessary to visit the place to realize the halo of love and admiration which has been thrown around it. Then it is also the centre of a famous angling district, and in 'Tibbie Shiel's' the 'contemplative man,' when his day of enjoyment is done, will find a tidy bed, and eke some jovial companion, who will make the evening hilarious as the day has been exhilarating. If the tourist has visited the *Grey Mare's Tail*, described in the preceding chapter, the same coach that has brought him from Moffat will bring him on to this scene of singular pastoral beauty.

St. Mary's Loch presents sufficient space to make up a fine landscape, and is not too large to be taken in at one glance. In its still beauty it has its chief charm:—

'You see that all is loneliness,
And silence aids—though the steep hills
Send to the lake a thousand rills,
In summer tide, so soft they weep,
The sound but lulls the ear to sleep.
Your horse's hoof-tread sounds too rude,
So stilly is the solitude.'

The square keep seen in the foreground is Dryhope Tower, the home of 'Mary Scott, the Flower of Yarrow.' Here we at once plunge into the old ballad and foray, for she married Wat of Harden,

a famed Border freebooter, and to name him is to let loose a flood
of reminiscences, legends, and family histories, on which the space
at command here will not permit us to enter.

The old kirk and kirkyard of St. Mary's were not less remarkable
than the loch:—

> 'Lord William was buried in St. Marie's Kirk,
> Lady Margaret in Marie's Quire.
> Out o' the lady's grave there grew a red rose
> And out o' the knight's a brier.'

Thus ends the tale of the *Douglas Tragedy*. Less famous people
are buried there, as another voice tells us,

> · For though, in feudal strife a foe
> Hath laid our lady's chapel low,
> Yet still beneath the hallowed soil
> The peasant rests him from his toil,
> And, dying, bids his bones be laid
> Where erst his simple fathers prayed.'

The river Yarrow flows through St. Mary's Loch, having passed
through the small Loch o' the Lowes before reaching the larger
water, 'Tibbie Shiel's' lying between the two lochs. Yarrow is well
known to every reader of Wordsworth, and we must pass rapidly
over what might be suggested by that single word, so soft in sound,
so suggestive of the old-world lore of this magical district. Of
every nook and dell, hill and valley, stream and loch, there are
stories and songs without end, everywhere

> 'You hear sweet melodies
> Attuned to some traditionary tale.'

Heroes and bold outlaws, fair women and sorrowing widows, strifes
and plunderings, genealogies and traditions—the Vale of Yarrow
and its surrounding hills and streams abound in these. All hushed
are they now, and the once warlike burgh of Selkirk is a thriving
manufacturing town, but while the 'Flowers o' the Forest' are, in
one sense 'a' wede away,' the natural attractiveness of the district
remains, with all the stories of byegone times to add to its interest
for romantic or poetic minds.

DUDDINGSTON LOCH.

THE smallest of all the notable lochs in Scotland, its circumfe-
rence being under a mile and a half, Duddingston is neverthe-
less famous as the resort of curlers and skaters, and for very many
years it has been a favourite playground of the citizens of Edinburgh,
whenever John Frost holds reign, and the ice is pronounced safe
by the police. The water is deep, and the loch is fed by several
springs far down in its depths, so that it is not a mere touch of
frost that will produce practicable ice at that part of the loch just
under the rocky knoll overhanging the middle. But when the frost
has lasted for two or three days, and the word is passed round in
the city that 'Duddingston is bearing,' then as if by common con-
sent the city is stirred to wend its way to the loch. Everyone is
there, from the arab who has perhaps at no other time a shoe on
his feet, and whose sport can only consist of 'keeping the pot boiling'
down the long slides that speedily get formed, to grave lawyers,
councillors and magistrates, while crowds of the fair sex also don
their skates, and anon the surface of the loch gets obscured by the
multitudes of people disporting on the ice. There have been times
when Duddingston, like the Thames, has been so strongly frozen
that an ox has been roasted upon it, and 'Frost Fair' is still a
tradition amongst old people. But a thickness of five or six inches
of ice suffices to make the entire surface safe and solid, and when
by the continuance of frost the ice reaches to nigh two feet thick
—no uncommon event—then the frosty carnival is at its best.

The village of Duddingston reposes under the wing of Arthur's
Seat—the hill shewn in our view—and lies to the right. In the

village is the house in which Prince Charles Edward lodged before
the battle of Prestonpans.   In former times, Duddingston was famous
for 'sheep's head' dinners, and its fruit gardens were also a favourite
resort in summer.   The parish church, seen amidst the bare trees,
is of architectural interest because of several portions of Norman
work still extant, and also from the fact that at the gate of the
churchyard are to be seen the 'jougs' an iron collar used as a
pillory, and also a curious relic, a 'loupin' on stane,' placed con-
siderately there so that persons attending church on horseback should
reach their saddle with the least trouble.   In the comfortable manse,
which lies away to the right, there lived for a time the Rev. John
Thomson, one of Scotland's greatest landscape painters, who was
minister of the parish, and died there in 1840.   The roadway running between the rocky knoll and the main hill is called the 'Windy
Gowl,' and in certain directions of the wind is almost impassable.
The precipitous rocks standing to the left of the hill are known as
'Samson's Ribs,' and consist of basaltic columns of the same formation as Fingal's Cave and the Giant's Causeway.   Viewed as we
see it from the east end of Duddingston Loch, Arthur's Seat loses
the fine leonine form it presents in every other direction.   It is a
noble hill, and although little more than eight hundred feet high,
its position as a solitary eminence gives it much grandeur of appearance, and the view from its summit is nowhere surpassed.   On
a clear day, the eye may wander from the Cheviot Hills on the
Border, to the Grampians in the north-west, and while the city of
Edinburgh lies spread out below, the varied landscape of the Lothians
and the sparkling waters of the Frith of Forth come in to make
up a panorama of varied beauty, amply repaying the slight toil of
the ascent.

LINLITHGOW LOCH.

WE reach here a quiet loch, of no great extent, but presenting a beauty of its own, and famous from its association with the ancient palace that crowns the peninsula in its centre. The tale of Flodden Field is closely associated with this palace, for in the small turret at the right hand corner furthest in our view there sat Queen Margaret in her bower, watching the turn of the road by which the king ought to be seen on his return, and weeping in secret misgiving as to the result of an enterprise which had been preceded by such a singular warning. The scene described by Lindsay of Pitscottie, and better known through 'Sir David Lindsay's Tale' in *Marmion*, took place in the old parish church, closely adjoining the palace, the square tower of which is seen over the trees. The king was in the practise, on each anniversary of his father's death, to proceed to St. Katherine's aisle,—still shown—and there to manifest his contrition for the share he had had in that sad act. When

'In Katherine's aisle the monarch knelt
With sackcloth shirt and iron belt
And eyes with sorrow streaming,

there stepped out from the crowd a mysterious stranger, 'in azure gown with cincture white,' who warned the king not to go to the intended war, more especially warning him, if he went, to guard himself against

'Woman fair
Her witching wiles and wanton snare.'

Every one knows that as regards both branches of the warning, the king proved regardless, and much of the disastrous result of Flodden arose from the king's fatal dalliance with a renowned Border lady.

Of the loch itself there is not much to say, after it has been told that it is dominated on the north by the gentle and verdant declivity of *Glower-o'er-em* or Bonnytoun Hill, on the summit of which is an elegant open gothic cross to the memory of Adrian Hope, a soldier of note who fell in the Indian mutiny. An exceedingly pleasant hour or two may be spent boating on the loch. On the level sward to the left of our view, the Linlithgow youth may be seen practising the game of cricket, for which use of the palace precincts leave is given. The palace grounds are open to the public, the building being in government hands, and, it is believed, swallowing up the whole rent of the small farm adjoining in the plasterers account for maintenance of the extensive ruins.

Within those walls the beautiful Mary Queen of Scots was born in 1542, and the room is shown, roofless and bare, as are other apartments of more or less interest. The newest part of the structure is on the north side, which is also the most ruinous, for when Hawley's dragoons, in 1746, set fire to the palace, the wooden floors here proved of course more easily destroyed than the vaulted and tiled floors in the older parts.

The porch, it may be mentioned, is copied at Abbotsford, and the fine fountain which stands in ruins in the courtyard has been reproduced in fac-simile at Holyrood Palace in Edinburgh. Leading to the palace from the town, the church door being also within it, is a fine gateway, with sculptured panels shewing the four knightly 'Orders' held by James V., namely, the Thistle, the Garter, the Golden Fleece, and St. Michael. The town of Linlithgow is a quiet, decayed county town, famous in history for the assassination of Regent Murray by Hamilton of Bothwellhaugh, in the High Street, and once distinguished by its singularly copious water supply from wells or springs, some of which still run on the streets, though most are now led into pipes for a general supply.

CORRA LINN.

THE old rhyme has it that three of the finest rivers in Scotland
set out to run a race, with varying fortunes:—

> 'The Tweed, the Annan and the Clyde,
> A' took their rise out o' ae hill side,
> Tweed ran, Annan wan,
> Clyde fell and brak its neck o'er Corra Linn.'

As an actual fact those three rivers find their head waters within a
very narrow space. Annan, with the shortest course, falls into the
Solway Firth; Tweed, getting many famous waters to strengthen its
current, the Gala, the Yarrow, the Ettrick and the Teviot, rolls its
noble course to the Border city of Berwick, and runs into the
German Ocean. The Clyde, after surviving its leap over Corra Linn
and other falls, becomes the great highway for ships at Glasgow,
and has the most useful, as well as the most romantic career of the
three.

Before it breaks its neck o'er Corra Linn, the Clyde has already
met with an accident at Bonnington Linn, and rushes over rocks
and gullies of the most hazardous kind, so that it reaches the
greater fall in a condition of turmoil and agitation far removed from
the gentle character of its earlier course. Above Bonnington,

> 'Smooth to the shelving brink, a copious flood
> Rolls fair and placid,'

but when it approaches Corra Linn, the water is alive and tumul-
tuous, and plunges over really as if it would break its neck in its
mad career.

To reach this fall, the visitor leaves the burgh of Lanark at its
lower end, proceeds to Kirkfieldbank, and there obtains a card of

admission to the grounds of Corehouse. The river is crossed at
Kirkfieldbank, but long ere reaching this the water has quieted
down, and flows gently along. The roar of Corra Linn may however be heard, especially if the Clyde be in flood. The walk after
entering the grounds is not long, when, following the course indicated by cards (though the sound of the water indicates the way
pretty well,) we reach the ruins of Corra Castle, just overhanging
the fall. A little roadway,—quite safe, for it is on the solid rock—
leads down to a projecting cliff from which, seated on the benches
placed there for the purpose, the splendid sight can be viewed at
leisure.

> 'Dashed in a cloud of foam, it sends aloft
> A living mist and forms a ceaseless shower.'

In the sun, tiny rainbows form, as different points of view are taken.
The deafening roar of this grand cataract rises and falls in a singular way, as if every slight inequality in the volume of the river
could be detected. The note is low and grand, so that the sound
of the human voice, shrilly set above its deep diapason, is easily
heard, and conversation can be quietly carried on. As in all great
waterfalls, the impression is deepened and strengthened by familiarity.
For one minute the feeling may arise 'is that all'—the next, the
grandeur of the scene has won its way to the mind and taken cap-
tive the imagination. Sit for an hour and the feeling will grow,
while to revisit it day after day for a week will intensify wonder
and admiration at the marvellous scene. Does it plunge and roar
thus, year in, year out, day and night, continuously? Is there no
pause, no rest, for the tost and troubled water—no quietness for
those reverberating rocks that stand around in awe of the ceaseless
and giant power that has so eaten its way into their hearts?

Everyone who visits Corra Linn walks through the ground to
Bonnington Linn, which from the Corehouse side is seen in face,
the water plunging over in two streams divided by an island. If
these falls are approached on the Bonnington side, the visitor sees
Corra Linn in face, can descend (by a steep descent) to the bed
right under the fall, visits the Wallace Cave where the river roars
through a gulley only a few feet wide, and may cross by an iron
bridge to the island in the middle of Bonnington Linn.

STONEBYRES FALL.

IN this cataract, the Clyde leaps a greater distance than in either
of the falls above, and by many it is considered the finer of the
two great waterfalls. It lies about three miles below Lanark, and
is reached from the public road. It is difficult of access, for the
visitor must either content himself with a distant view, or take his
heart in his hand and descend a precipitous and dangerous path,
where at times to hang on by the eyelids may seem the only re-
source. In speaking of Corra Linn, nothing has been said of the
extreme beauty of the scene through which the river flows. From
Hamilton to some distance above Lanark, the Clyde valley is a
famous fruit district, itself a testimony to the richness and mildness
of the locality. It would be vain to dwell on the sylvan splendours
of the reach of the river from Bonnington to below Corra Linn.
High banks overhang the whole way, sometimes running to bold
cliffs, crowned with woody knolls, with shining snatches of verdure
in every crevice; at other points wooded to the water's edge.
Standing on the bridge at Kirkfieldbank the river is seen pleasantly
flowing on towards its third leap, the greatest of the series. Before
passing by the road to this scene a detour should be made, on the
opposite bank, to the Cartland Crags, where a lofty bridge crosses
the river Mouse, and amongst whose lofty cliffs the hero William
Wallace found refuge after his famous exploit in slaying Haselrig
the English Sheriff.

Approaching Stonebyres, the war of troubled waters is again heard.
The stream is not far off the road, and only a short walk is necessary
before the scene bursts upon the view. Of course glimpses of the

waterfall can be obtained from many points, but the choice aspect is to reach the bed of the stream below, and gaze upwards on the mighty rush of waters. To one who is bold and sure-footed there is no great difficulty in approaching pretty near the fall, unless the river should be in spate, when of course the difficulty is increased, and may indeed become too dangerous to be possible. Supposing the fall approached within several score of yards, what a splendid scene, and how thrilling is that on which we gaze!

> 'O what an amphitheatre surrounds
> The abyss, in which the downward mass is plunged,
> Stunning the ear.'

The entire descent is about ninety feet, in several distinct leaps. This broken character of the two great falls gives them a great deal of their distinctive beauty. Doubtless, if the flood had plunged in one sheer leap, the turmoil below would have been greater, but the picturesque aspects of the scene would have been lessened. The jutting rocks and ragged edges by which the fall is broken, give to the face of the waterfall an ever varying feature, and with the undulating flow and gamut of sound here, as at Corra Linn, it presents at each moment some new point for admiration. Then the triple and repeated leaps churn the water into the snowiest foam and spray, so that the falls have great brightness and lightness in spite of the quantity of water plunging over. The combination of tones of colour is indeed notable, and when to the greens and browns of rock and tree, and the white foam of the fall, there is added a brilliant sunshine and cerulean sky flecked with light clouds, anyone standing here may well exclaim that

> 'Earth hath not anything to show more fair.'

LOCH LEVEN.

THIS loch has at the present day a two-fold attraction—historical and piscatorial. Like most other places of interest in Scotland, the story of Loch Leven and its castle clings round the chequered career of Mary Queen of Scots. Here, for eleven months, the beautiful Stuart Queen lay a prisoner, and eventually her escape was arranged with all the romantic devotion and quiet daring with which she was ever able to inspire all who fell under the spell of her charms or the pity of her fate. Here, as Burns has taught us to believe, she uttered that sad 'Lament on the Approach of Spring' which forms one of the most touching bits of the national poet's writings,

> 'Now Nature hangs her mantle green
> On every blooming tree.
> And spreads her sheets of daisies white
> Out o'er the grassy lea.
>   *   *   *   *   *
> Now blooms the lily by the bank,
> The primrose down the brae;
> The hawthorn's budding in the glen,
> And milk-white is the slae:
> The meanest hind in fair Scotland
> May rove their sweets amang,
> But I, the Queen of a' Scotland,
> Maun lie in prison strang.'

The waters encompassing the castle form a loch of an irregular square form, with a maximum length of four miles, and over two miles wide. The island on which the castle stands is not the largest, there being, at the eastern end, a large island named after St. Serf, and still showing the remains of a priory, originally Culdee, and of which Wyntoun, author of the *Orygynale Cronykil*, was once the head. The castle, a massive square keep, with a quadrangle of fortified buildings around it, is of great antiquity, dating, it is alleged, from Pictish times. The walls of the keep are in good preservation, and the lower floors, being vaulted, still remain. The surrounding wall, with circular towers, can be walked upon, but the main buildings in the area are only indicated by lines of foundation walls. From the side nearest in our view a sunken causeway formerly connected the castle with the promontory on which Kinross House stands, and it can still be traced at the bottom of the loch.

The surroundings of the loch include the Western Lomond, and the Bishop Hill on the north-west, and Benarty on the south. Regarding the last named hill, a retired politician is said to have written the following couplet, in retirement here,

> 'Oh blest is the man wha belangs to nae party
> But sits at his door and glowers at Benarty.'

The district traversed in reaching the loch impresses the visitor as being fruitful and prosperous, and there are abundant evidences around of much mineral wealth. It is, however, for angling purposes that Loch Leven attracts the greater number of its visitors. The Loch Leven trout are active and firm-fleshed, and are in much esteem both for the sport they yield and for the table. At the west end of the loch, close by the town of Kinross, boats are let for angling, and besides many private parties, a large number of clubs hold stated competitions on Loch Leven, and the 'baskets' made, and the prospects of sport, are the subject of daily reports in the Edinburgh and Glasgow newspapers. Beds and boats are telegraphed for in advance, regarding which a good story is told of an Edinburgh journalist, once famous with rod and line, who first sent a wire to the unsophisticated Kinrossians. When he arrived he saw that he was unexpected, and asked 'did you not get my message?' The reply was, 'Ou ay, we got a letter, but as it *wasna in your ain handwriting*, we paid nae attention to it!'

LOCH FAD.

THIS is one of the lochs without a history, although doubtless men have lived and died, married and given in marriage, laboured, plotted, and perhaps thieved and robbed upon its borders. It owes its presence in our collection because of its position in an island, and that one of the most tempting spots in the more low-land parts of Scotland. The island of Bute, which unites with Arran and the Greater and Lesser Cumbraes to make up a county to which Bute gives its name, lies on the west of the Frith of Clyde, and is separated from the mainland on the inner side by a narrow, tortuous, and picturesque channel called the Kyles of Bute. Landing at Rothesay we find a busy, cleanly, charming watering place, with suburbs of Craigmore and Port Bannatyne filling up the lovely shores of Rothesay Bay, and giving from every window en-chanting peeps of water and hill, carrying the view far into the mountainous county of Argyle. Writing of this lovely, verdant island, David Macbeth Moir (the *Delta* of Blackwood,) says

'each moment brought
A new creation to the eye of thought.'

So much for poetry. We may tell of Bute a more prosaic story, when a town-lady, going, as the Glasgow people say, 'doon the watter,' asked a lodging-house keeper in Rothesay about thunder, and received the very satisfactory rejoinder, *more Scottice*, in question form, 'Wha ever heard o' thunder in an island?'

Leaving Rothesay by the road near its centre, and passing the parish kirk, Loch Fad is found about two miles out. On the south

side, forming the foreground and left of our view, the shores are
low and green, but on the other side it swells out into bolder out-
lines, and may fitly claim to be a Highland loch. A curious mound
crosses the water, leading to its northern side. On this side of the
pretty island loch, Edmund Kean, in 1827, built himself a residence.
From his windows, and more especially from a summer-house placed
on the height above, there is a grand view, embracing not only
the near waters of Loch Fad, but glimpses of Rothesay Bay, and
on the outer line the bold features of Argyleshire. Over the door-
way of this summer-house, the great tragedian had those lines

> 'How glorious from the loopholes of retreat
> To peep at such a world.'

And this concisely expresses the feeling with which a wearied man
may seek his holiday in such an island as this. True it is, that
Rothesay has a telegraph, and a post office, and a newspaper, and
that in two hours' time one can be set down in the heart of Glasgow.
But the insular charm is a great one.

> 'The promises of blooming spring live here,
> And all the blessings of the ripening year.'

Those lines were formerly inscribed at Mount Stuart House, the
residence of the Marquis of Bute, recently burnt and rebuilt. It
lies on the Clyde shore of the island, at no great distance from
Rothesay,—indeed there are no *great* distances anywhere in the
island—and forms one of the many beautiful drives through the
island. On the way thither the village of Ascog is passed, where on
a rocky point jutting out into the river there is a little church, and
at its end a monument to Montagu Stanley, poet, actor, artist, at
one time well known in Edinburgh society. From Mount Stuart
and Ascog, and the other houses on this side of the island, there
is an extensive view of the Frith of Clyde, on the broad waters of
which there is a never-ending panorama of steamers, yachts, and
gallant vessels.

.

LOCH LOMOND.

JUSTLY termed the Queen of the Scottish Lochs, this magnificent sheet of water presents an almost infinite variety of scenery. It has on the eastern side one of Scotland's notable mountains, Ben Lomond, and around are hills of lesser, though still great altitude, over which the giant mountain towers as a monarch amidst his courtiers. There are on the loch several excellent steamers, and as the distance from the pier at Balloch to the landing place at Ardlui is upwards of twenty miles, a day can be delightfully spent in going and returning, giving the charms of Highland scenery without the ordinary fatigues of travelling, and the delights of an excursion on a wide expanse of water without the attendant risk of sea-sickness.

There are on the bosom of Loch Lomond several large islands, and many small islets, adding greatly to the beauty and variety of its scenery. Some of the islands are clad in oak; one is called Inchlonaig, or yew-tree island; some display the silvery leafage of the birch, others are covered with the hardier fir, and here again the element of variety comes in to charm the sense. Our view shews the loch before it has narrowed to the lesser channel between Inversnaid and Ardlui, and before it has lost the charm of those wooded islands that beautify the southern and wider part. The bulky form of Ben Lomond fills up the scene, and the sun shining amidst clouds is significant of the varied weather that may be encountered in one day. The wide reaches and more lowland aspects of the southern end may be passed in all the enjoyment of a noon-day summer sun, but ere the upper part of the loch is reached clouds may gather, and a sudden torrent of rain or a sullen blast of wind may overtake the voyager. But again, in an hour all is peaceful and beautiful, and the rain has served to augment and enhance the burns, rivulets, and streams, whose crystal waters feed the loch from every shore. On several of the islands are ruins of old castles, and all around the scene is redolent of memories of old feuds, violent strifes, and fierce clan struggles. To-day all this is changed, and we revel only in the grandeur and beauty of the scene. Those caves hide no caterans to rob us, the cattle and sheep on hill or island are safe from the foray, and the dwellers around pay no black mail to save themselves from the attentions of stout and bare-legged ruffians.

At Rowardennan Inn are guides and ponies, and although the stalwart man may dispense with the latter, it is not safe to attempt the ascent of Ben Lomond without a guide familiar with the road, for sudden mists may envelop the climber, and a mistake in the road may lead to death. What is to be seen from the top? Rather ask what is not seen? Right away to 'the back of the North Wind' stretch the innumerable hills. To the west the mountain ranges of Argyleshire, to the south-west the long peninsula of Cantyre, with the waters of the Atlantic seen beyond; to the east the castles of Stirling and Edinburgh may be picked out, to the south the busy Clyde, and in the foreground the splendid loch itself. Ben Lomond stands as a sentinel or outer-guard to the Highlands, and hence the range of view from it is of unusual extent. All that is to be seen from it cannot be described, so rich, so extensive, so varied are the prospects presented.

It is said that last century a visitor wrote some lines on a window-pane at Tarbet Inn, on the ascent of Ben Lomond, and a few words of his advice may fitly close our essay:—

> Rest, oh! rest—long, long upon the top,
> There 'hale the breezes, nor with toilsome haste
> Down the rough slope thy youthful vigour waste.
> So shall thy wondering sight at once survey,
> Woods, lakes and mountains, valleys, rocks and sea,
> Huge hills that heaped in crowded order stand,
> Stret 'ed o'er the western and the northern land.

FALLS OF INVERSNAID.

AN essential part of the Trosachs tour is the coach drive between Inversnaid on Loch Lomond, and Stronachlacher pier, where the steamer on Loch Katrine begins (or ends) her journey. There is one little loch on the way, from which emerges the Arklet, which runs into Loch Lomond, and forms the fine series of cascades of which the upper fall is shown in our view. There is almost no need to waste words in any description of this delightful scene, so well does the picture we present describe itself. We may say of it, in lines that Wordsworth has linked indissolubly with the place

> 'A very shower
> Of beauty is thy earthly dower
>   *   *   *   *
> These trees, a veil just half withdrawn,
> This fall of water, that doth make
> A murmur near the silent lake.
>   *   *   *   *
> In truth together do ye seem
> Like something fashioned in a dream.'

It may well be doubted whether the Highland girl, with her 'twice seven consenting years,' and her 'homely ways and dress,' would have enchained the sympathetic poet, had he seen her in some place less lovely, or less provocative of a feeling of poetic contentment. Be that as it may, it will be confessed that the scene, with or without a 'Highland Girl' to stir the strings of the heart, will remain impressed on the mind of every one who is sensible of the beautiful. And so we can join with Wordsworth, in the conclusion he arrives at, always excepting, if necessary, his passion for the girl of fourteen—

> For I, methinks, till I grow old
> As fair before me shall behold,
> As I do now, the cabin small,
> The lake, the bay, the waterfall,
> And thee, the spirit of them all!'

There are many remembrances of Rob Roy, truthful some of them, fanciful the rest, in the vicinity of Inversnaid. Not far off is Rob Roy's Cave, the entrance scarcely visible, while within there is a vast cavern, whence in fancy we may descry

> 'The wild Macgregor's savage clan
> Emerging at their chieftain's call
> To foray or to festival.'

On the road between Loch Lomond and Loch Katrine is seen Inversnaid Fort, now in ruins, having in itself a chequered history. Built in 1713 to check the Macgregors, it is said to have been at one time resided in by General Wolfe. Now, like some doomed city of old, 'the cormorant and the bittern possess it,' for the Macgregors are at peace, their name and tartan are no longer proscribed, and now no black-mail is levied on any one in the district but the strangers, and for their protection the government has no need to provide. It is at times a costly thing to travel in the Highlands, when beds are at a ransom, and all the wealth of Ind will not secure the coveted box seat of the coach. But a Macgregor who levies black-mail in a Scottish city has put the thing in a nutshell, for when remonstrated with about his charges he said, 'What for should I charge less?—my hoose is fu' every nicht!' There is true political economy shaking hands with the plunderer of the Saxon!

LOCH KATRINE.

THE most brilliant gem in the loch scenery of Scotland is un-
questionably Loch Katrine or Ketturin, and it is needful, however attractive or deserving of praise other waters may have proved,
to avoid exhausting upon them the vocabulary of praise, lest no
words of greater admiration should be left for this, the loveliest of
them all. Even if Scott had not superadded to Loch Katrine the
witchery of his genius, and made Ellen's Isle as famous among the
abodes of heroines as the Fountain of Vaucluse, this water would
have asserted its claim to public regard. True, it was Scott that
gave the impetus for touring in Scotland—or Scott-land as some
have called it!—and Loch Katrine thus obtained a first hold upon
the admiration of the world. But spite of all rivals, it maintains
first rank, and although it cannot cope with Loch Lomond or Loch
Maree in point of size, neither of those great lochs command the
same admiration.

Scott in *The Lady of the Lake,* has depicted the scene in words
of fire; taking sunset for the time. The 'gallant grey' has fallen,
—the guides still point out the very spot!—and the huntsman pursues his way till the end of the glen is reached, and Loch Katrine
bursts on his view,

> 'An airy point he won,
> Where, gleaming with the setting sun
> One burnished sheet of living gold,
> Loch Katrine lay beneath him rolled,
> In all her length far winding lay
> With promontory, creek and bay,
> And islands that, empurpled bright
> Floated amid the livelier light,
> And mountains that like giants stand,
> To sentinel enchanted land.'

F

In pointing to 'promontory, creek, and bay,' as the characteristics of the loch, Scott has depicted its most charming attributes, while the islands, of which Ellen's Isle is the largest, help to enhance the effect. As the little steamer breaks the still waters into drops that glance like gems in the sunlight, the scene changes every moment, —changes in detail, but never in degree of beauty, for the loch is lovely throughout, and never fails to enchant the eye.

The chief attraction of the loch itself is the lovely wooded isle that fills the foreground of our view,

> 'The wild rose, eglantine, and broom,
> Wasted around their rich perfume.
> The birch trees wept in fragrant balm,
> The aspens slept beneath the calm,
> The silver light, with quivering glance
> Play'd on the water's still expanse.'

Seldom indeed will the casual visitor have the opportunity of viewing this scene thus, by the silvery moonlight. But in sunlight it is not less beautiful, and the description is complete. Next to the island, the point of attraction is the 'silver strand,' from whence one of the many fine views of Ben Venne may be had.

While Loch Katrine thus ministers to our love for the beautiful, its waters have learned to combine the *utile* with the *dulce*, and here, in October 1859, came Queen Victoria to turn on the water for the supply of Glasgow. Many and fierce were the controversies as to this scheme. But Lord Provost Stewart, who was mercilessly assailed for upholding such a costly scheme of water supply, is now commemorated in Glasgow by a splendid fountain in the West-End Park, and staticians and sanitary reformers are able to show that the death rate amongst the half million crowded workers in Glasgow has manifestly lessened since the city acquired the right to drink the sparkling waters of Loch Katrine.

LOCH LUBNAIG.

TURNING aside from the formal round of the Trosachs and Loch Lomond, to penetrate into that wonderful district which the Callander and Oban railway has opened up, we reach, at no great distance from Callander, Loch Lubnaig, 'the crooked lake,' so called from its bent form, which is almost identical with the form of the boomerang. The river Leny, which drains the lake, passes through the Pass of Leny, once famous as a gateway defending the entrance to the Highlands. Here, whether viewed from the train or the road, the river is seen to rush over huge rocks, tearing, roaring, and tumbling, in a manner calculated to terrify the timid entrant to this wild district.

The lake itself lies clear, black, and deep, a somewhat sullen, yet always beautiful sheet of water. On the left the dark masses of Ben Ledi cast their shadows upon the water, intensifying the depth of its tone, and giving the loch its distinctive character. Near the water the banks are in many places full of gentle woodland beauty, but as a rule the impression made by the overhanging bulk and the dusky-hued rocks of Ben Ledi, absorb the sense, and the loch ever presents an idea of grandeur and desolation. The railway line follows the edge of the loch over its whole length, and the construction of this track formed a most difficult engineering task, which at some stages of its progress was nigh abandoned in despair. To get round the hard and unyielding shoulders of the mountain, where they impinged direct upon the water, embankments had to be made across a number of bays and arms of the loch. In one case the task of throwing rocks and stones into the water was persevered in

for nine months without perceptible result, but by continued labour
a footing above water level was at last obtained. As the train
pursues its course along the bank of the lovely loch,—the eye the
while rejoicing in the dark and placid beauty of the water, and the
charm of the hill scenery beyond,—there will at times come the
feeling that the distance between the carriage window and the
treacherously pellucid depths of the loch is all too little. The fear
is unfounded, for no sign of subsidence has been shewn—the mass
of stones thrown in was too solid for that. But this is a feature
in the case that no traveller will fail to notice, and the impression
thus made by Loch Lubnaig makes it a water which once seen
will never be forgotten.

Near the debouchure of the river is St. Bride's Chapel, where
Angus thrust the fiery cross into the hands of Norman, as described
in *The Lady of the Lake.* About half-way up the loch is Ardchullary
farmhouse, which was at one time the retreat of Bruce the traveller
in Abyssinia, who here wrote the volumes on which a century ago
such keen controversies arose. On the opposite side, where the
railway runs, is Laggan, said to have been the abode of Helen
Macgregor, whom Rob Roy carried off from here by force and
married. In the veritable histories of Rob Roy, however, his wife's
name is given as Mary, daughter of Macgregor of Comar.

LOCH EARN.

NO one can accuse the Scottish lochs of want of variety, for in each is found some specialty, some individual beauty, that stamps it on the mind, so that the visitor can carry away a distinct impression. Nobody, for example, who has been at St. Fillans, or attended the annual games there, is likely to have any difficulty in remembering this pretty modern village, and the fine loch near which it lies. St. Fillan, it may be mentioned is a personage of great sanctity in Scottish hagiology. And when his crosier, carried away to Canada by its 'Dewar' or hereditary keeper, was recently restored to Scotland, and placed in the National Museum at Edinburgh, one might have almost doubted whether Scotland were really Protestant at all, so full was every one of the fame of this great miracle-working saint. As is well known, it was the presence of his arm-bone, in the hands of the Abbot of Inchaffray, which enabled the Scots to win the battle of Bannochburn!

Loch Earn, it is to be understood, was known before the Trosachs. Although shut in at its upper end by the gloomy hills that darken Glen Ogle, and from that side until recently not very accessible, it was reached from Crieff and St. Fillans, long before Scott invented those wondrous stories about the Trosachs district which are to-day so veritable that the scene of each incident is pointed out. And in its perfection of beauty—for so we consider it—it well deserves to hold its place in public regard. The reverse view from that given here is also beautiful, and it may be said that no more perfect scene can be witnessed than from the carriage window in the Oban train as, high on the side of a steep and terror-striking mountain, it enables the visitor to look down, as with a bird's-eye view, upon this lovely loch. The sheet of water is symmetrical, a feature which may be a beauty or a disadvantage, according as the spectator looks for completeness of display, or for mystery as the aim of the picturesque. But, as it is expressed by MacCulloch, Loch Earn is 'consistent and complete,' and he points out that by this completeness it possesses an appearance of extent beyond which it actually possesses. The mind can grasp it all, but we feel that there is a great deal to be grasped. The hills are sufficiently high to give dignity to the scene, and the glowing verdure all around gives it softness and beauty. Benvoirlich is its summit hill, and the house of Ardvoirlich—the 'Darlinvaroch' of Scott's *Legend of Montrose*—occupies a fine spot half way down the loch. In this mansion is preserved a singular talisman, a perfect sphere of rock crystal, with four silver bands, which throughout the country side has the credit of curing diseases when dipped in water to be drunk by the patient.

It remains to notice some physical peculiarities of this loch. Although situated at an elevation of several hundred feet above sea-level, its temperature is so equal that the water is never known to freeze, and even the stream that flows from it never shows ice on its surface till it has run several miles into bleaker regions. The depth of the water is at some places six hundred feet, and as it lies in the immediate region of earthquake in Scotland, it is allowable to conjecture that some hidden fire of nature far below keeps the water just a point or two above ordinary heat, and thus produces the phenomenon stated. There are trout in the loch, and leave to fish can readily be obtained at either end, as the hotel keepers have boats upon the loch.

LOCH TAY.

MANY of the lochs of which we have spoken have the advantage of Loch Tay as regards the number of their visitors, and their repute in distant parts. But in no case is greater beauty to be seen than here, and no spot in Scotland will more fully repay the labour of travelling to see it. It lies surrounded with splendid hills, Ben Lawers on the north proudly towering over the scene. It is very finely wooded over all its banks, and its slightly irregular form creates change and variety at every mile of the way. It is the merit of Loch Tay that now the visitor has 'three courses' before him, like a great statesman of our day. When he leaves Killin station at the upper end, or Aberfeldy station at the lower end, he may follow the coach route on the north side, or he may prefer the less public road on the south side, or he may sail on the bosom of the water in the steamer, the *Lady of the Lake*, launched in 1882 by the Earl of Breadalbane. From Killin, the direction of our view, the north road, which is generally followed, lies to the left. Just at the head of the road—one of the roads made by General Wade —is seen the ivy-covered ruin of Finlarig Castle, situated amidst fine woods, and having near it the burial place of the Breadalbane family. The Queen, visiting Taymouth Castle in 1842, lunched at Auchmore, where the south road strikes off. She speaks of the scene as enchanting, and it would be difficult to find a more appropriate word. Ben Lawers, the ascent of which is made from Lawers inn, has not many superiors in height in Scotland, and its ascent is not difficult, while the view from it is superb. Behind Ben Lawers, and further on running to a junction with the valley in which Loch Tay lies, is the grand district of Glen Lyon, of

which many think, that from its upper reaches in the Forest of
Mamlorn to where the Lyon falls into the Tay, there is not a glen
in Scotland so weird and yet so verdantly beautiful. The ascent of
Ben Lawers, it may be mentioned, has special charms for the botanist,
boasting amidst many rare plants the drooping saxifrage (*S. cernua,*)
not elsewhere found in this country. The district abounds in water
and in waterfalls, including the falls of Acharn, which are seen from
the north side, but may be visited if the south road be taken. From
near Aberfeldy, when the noble river Tay, the birth of this grand
loch, has run some miles of its course, the tourist naturally turns
aside to visit the falls of Moness, 'the epitome of waterfalls,' as
Pennant says, on a stream which flows through the town of Aberfeldy. Here is the scene so exquisitely sung by Burns;

> 'The braes ascend like lofty wa's
> The foaming stream, deep-roaring, fa's
> O'er hung wi' fragrant, spreading shaws,
>   The Birks o' Aberfeldy.'

Close by Kenmore, at the lower end of the loch is a wooded island,
on which lies buried Princess Sybilla, daughter of Henry I. and
wife of the Scots King, Alexander I. In the inn-parlour at Kenmore
Burns wrote some lines of intense feeling and adoration, in which
he dwells on

> 'The sweeping theatre of hanging woods;
> Th' incessant roar of headlong tumbling floods,'

—twin characteristics of this most attractive region.

LOCH AWE.

IT is but seldom that the eye can rest upon so much soft beauty and stern grandeur as can be seen at one moment in looking at this grand loch. Rivalling Loch Lomond in length, it is much narrower, and while richer, is perhaps less varied. In sailing over its clear waters, the richly wooded islands and green banks suggest some large and placid river. Crowded with islands, especially at its upper part, each one with its ruin, its legend, or its sylvan beauty to attract, the loch is in all respects charming. There is Inishail —the island of the fair, immortalized by Hamerton,—Inis-Fraoch, the Hesperides of Celtic romance, with golden fruit, a dragon, a lover, and a legend, all in due form, Inistrynich, the island of the Druids, and many others. And near the head of the loch is the peninsula on which stands Kilchurn Castle, to whom we may say with Wordsworth,

·thy hour of rest
Is come, and thou art silent in thy age.'

This ruin is one of the favourite subjects of the Scottish landscape painter, and its picturesque character is well seen in our view. Though now a complete wreck, it was entire and served as a post for the royal troops in the '45, and almost within living memory it was a habitable mansion. It is said that an economical steward of the Earl of Breadalbane fancied the roof timbers would be useful at Taymouth Castle, and had them removed. It is certain that for long the gigantic stronghold served as a common quarry for the surrounding district, and that even the church in the adjoining Glen Orchy has in it some stones from the old castle. On the high

F

ground to the right is a circular and somewhat rude yet effective stone monument to Duncan Ban Macintyre, of Glen Orchy, who died in Edinburgh in 1812, aged 89 years, and whose fame as a Gaelic poet is unique.

At its upper end the loch forks into two arms, that to the right receiving the Orchy and other feeders, while that to the left runs through the dark Pass of Brander, and there, in the river Awe, the loch finds its outlet. Formerly the saying that 'it's a far cry to Lochow' had more significance, for now the railway has made this grand loch easily accessible, and as the line skirts the upper end of the loch (where a large hotel has been built) and proceeds on terraced banks through the Pass of Brander, crossing the rapids of the Awe on a high bridge, the traveller enjoys the beauties of the district in a large degree. The sail on the loch is, however, a part of the Highland tour which no visitor should forego.

Ben Cruachan, whose double peak (the highest 3667 feet) dominates the district, is one of the most striking of the Scottish hills, in its massive form, magnificently swelling contours, and unique position, giving perhaps a greater idea of bulk than other hills of the same height. On three sides it rises from the water's edge, Loch Awe in its two upper branches, the river Awe, and Loch Etive, the sea-loch into which the latter runs, washing its base. The ascent of this noble Ben is best made from the Bridge of Awe, a scene rendered familiar in Scott's *Highland Widow*, and the view from the summit is magnificent. No one will ever regret the toil of surmounting

> 'yon sovereign lord
> Huge Cruachan, a thing that meaner hills
> Might crush, nor know that it had suffered harm.'

LOCH ETIVE.

COMING round the base of Ben Cruachan by rail, and leaving the Pass of Brander and the rapids of the river Awe, the observant traveller will not fail to notice that the large and spreading water he now approaches has the character of a sea loch. If no other indication were given, the presence of brown sea-wrack along the margin of the water would show that here the tides ebb and flow. Far away to the right, surrounded by grand hills, and closed in at the distance by the bulky shoulders of Buchael Etive, is the upper reach of the loch, forming in itself a most attractive portion of Highland scenery. The railway, however, confines itself solely to the south side of the lower and salter reach of the water, separated from the inner loch by a reef of rocks, through the chief opening in which the receding tide rushes with the character of a water-fall. Passing along the loch, there is seen on the north side the remains of Ardchattan Priory, one of the three religious houses established in Scotland after the pattern of those in the Val de Choux (Cabbage Valley, or, _Scottice_, Kale Glen, as the recent historian of Pluscardyn ingeniously puts it) near Chatillon, in Burgundy. Loch Etive narrows at its mouth at Connell Ferry, and then opens grandly into Loch Linnhe.

Dunstaffnage Castle, shown in the view, is one of the royal castles of the Duke of Argyle. The building, which is of great antiquity and strength, was destroyed by fire in 1715. Some guns supposed to have belonged to the Spanish Armada are in the castle, and the remains of a chapel are seen, in which are supposed to rest, not only the remains of the actual King Alexander II, but of various more or less apocryphal Dalriad kings. Over the water is shown the site of the Pictish capital of Beregonium, (said to have been destroyed by fire from heaven!) and, near it, on Bal-an-righ, is a vitrified hill fort, the *Selma* of the poems of Ossian.

At Dunstaffnage was at one time kept the Coronation Stone, or Stone of Destiny, of which the tradition says that it was the veritable stone on which Jacob laid his head when he had the dream on his way to Padan-Aram! Geologists say that the structure of the *Lia Fail* agrees with that of the stones at Dunstaffnage. Leaving out tradition, the stone is said to have been removed from this place to Scone, near Perth, where the kings of Scotland continued to be crowned till Edward Longshanks removed this Scottish palladium to Westminster Abbey, where it remains to-day, fixed beneath the coronation chair. It is said that Edward II. was willing to restore the Stone of Destiny to Scotland, but was prevented by the London mob. The 'destiny' was proclaimed in verses that have been rendered in this form

'Unless the fates are faithless grown
And prophets' voice be vain
Where'er is found this sacred stone
The Scottish race shall reign.'

Without a doubt, the house of Brunswick claims the throne of those realms in consequence of their Stuart descent, so that the stone has not as yet failed in its effect, and every one desires that the 'destiny' should continue in the same line, whether the boulder from the borders of Loch Etive has anything to do with the matter or not.

THE FALLS OF FOYERS.

HERE we have the culmination, as regards beauty, of the water-falls of Scotland. This is one of the scenes that struck the imagination of Burns, as, standing by the fall, he wrote in pencil words that can never be omitted in any description for they fulfil all that description can effect—

'Among the heathy hills and rugged woods
The roaring Foyers pours his mossy floods
Till full he dashes on the rocky mounds
Where thro' a shapeless breach his stream resounds
As high in air the bursting torrents flow
As deep recoiling surges foam below
Prone down the rock the whitening sheet descends
And viewless Echo's ear, astonished, rends:
Dim seen through rising mists and ceaseless showers
The hoary cavern, wide surrounding, lowers.
Still, thro' the gap the struggling river toils
And still, below, the horrid cauldron boils.'

The last idea is one that ever recurs in the presence of a great waterfall, and in every respect the description is perfect, the shape-less breach, the bursting torrent and the deep recoiling surges are each impressed on the mind, even if the visitor has not read Burns's lines. When Dr. Johnson visited Scotland, he too saw the Fall of 'Fiers' as it is called in his *Journey to the Western Islands*, and although a long continuance of dry weather had robbed the fall of much of its promised grandeur, Dr. Johnson, while philosophically remarking that 'Nature never gives everything at once,' gives a striking word-picture, exercising as he says, his thoughts to 'conceive the effect of a thousand streams poured from the mountains into one channel, struggling for expansion in a narrow passage, exasperated by rocks rising in their way and at last discharging all their violence of waters by a sudden fall through the horrid chasm.' This is splendid, and if old Samuel Johnson had seen Foyers at its best he could not have improved on the description.

The steamers on Loch Ness invariably stay at the pier of Foyers, affording time to walk to the grand falls. The hotel here is built on the site of 'General's Hut,' and still in Johnson's day it is 'not ill stocked with provisions.' The name is given because General Wade, when superintending those roads that are rendered famous by his epitaph, was lodged at this spot. There are two falls, with a distance of about a quarter of a mile between them, the lower or great fall being that shown in the view. Over the upper fall there is a light bridge thrown, and the scene here is very fine, though it is exceeded in grandeur by the snow-white rush of the lower waterfall. The latter earns its title of the 'fall of smoke,' the spray rising in never-ceasing clouds of grey mist-like smoke.

A notable scene in the immediate vicinity of Foyers is the Pass of Inverfarigaig, with vast cliffs, and many interesting geological points of study. By ascending this pass and striking westward a fine approach can be obtained to the upper fall of Foyers. Again, by a ferry near the pier, the loch can be crossed, and the quaintly shaped hill of Mealfourvonie can be ascended. Again, a short distance brings the visitor to Castle Urquhart, while a little further on is Drumnadrochit, rendered famous by *Punch's* Fat Contributor, —'your health sir, in a dram!'—where but for the telegraph wire, and the post office, and the newspaper, and the frequent steamboats, a man might moon away his time, and never tire of the fine air, the wonderful surroundings, and the remote stillness. If a man wished to be a hermit, and yet see much of the world, to be unoccupied, yet never fail of variety of occupation, to be rested and refreshed, yet interested and employed, he could not do better than take up his abode at Foyers for the four or five months of the long days between April and October.

LOCH NESS.

THIS loch, with soundings deeper than any in the German Ocean, has come into notice in an especial manner, because it forms, in its twenty-four miles, a large section of famous tourist route, the Caledonian Canal. The loch is within a few miles of the handsome town of Inverness; the river Ness, draining the loch, running through the town to the Moray Frith after a short but lovely course over the intervening distance. Between Loch Ness and the outlet there lies a vast gravel peninsula, dividing the section known as Loch Doch-four from the rest, the barricade thus formed being a safeguard to the town against the enormous pressure of water that would other-wise flow out in times of flood. As it is, the records of the town point to terrible devastations from the Ness coming down in strength. The deep waters of the loch get lashed into stormy waves by gusts of wind rushing down from the surrounding glens, so that Loch Ness does not always present the peaceful aspect of our view, as seen by the summer visitor. But we will take it on such a day by preference, and can warrant to every one who comes that the sail in the fine steamers plying on the loch and canal will be redolent of joy and beauty and grandeur. We may conceive that there is more comfort and ease in seeing Loch Ness than when, a hundred and nine years ago Johnson and Boswell rode along its shores. But the high terms in which Bozzy speaks of the scene are as fresh to-day as then, for the road shaded with birch trees, the hills above it, the 'sequestered and agreeably wild' scene, are as fitted to engross attention as ever. We know also that they would see Castle Urquhart, on its prominent peninsula, and would probably be struck by the notable form of the hill called Mealfourvonie. They stopped at the 'General's Hut,' as indeed we all do, for the new hotel at Foyers is built on its site, whence we take the road to visit the falls of that name, as described elsewhere.

Fort Augustus, standing at the western end of the loch, is now a Benedictine monastery and school. Built after the Jacobite rising in 1715, as part of the plan for holding the turbulent Highlanders in subjection, it remained crown property for a century and a half, and falling into disuse and neglect was then sold for its present purpose.

Although our view gives but a small section of the loch, our notice may be directed to the other parts of the route that now yearly carries thousands of tourists through the Glenmore-nan-Albin. There is at Corpach the famous 'Neptune's staircase,' where eight locks bring the boat from the outer loch to the canal level. Loch Lochy, ten miles in length, forms the western portion. Then after two miles of canal Loch Oich is reached, this sheet of water being four miles long. Then another cut takes to Loch Ness, the whole distance, from the staircase to Muirton lock on the east side being about fifty miles. The entire route, barring the delay at the locks up and down, has all the charm of one continuous voyage on an inland lake, the portions in canal being almost indistinguishable except in width from the natural channels. There is a constant variety and glory of scenery during the day's sail, and nowhere can the traveller spend a holiday with more delightful surroundings.

LOCH CORUISK.

THERE are few scenes more fitted to move the imagination than the wonderful loch, and the more wonderful hills that surround it, presented in this view. It is somewhat of an exaggeration for Sir Walter Scott to say that here

'Nor tree, nor shrub, nor plant, nor flower,
Nor ought of vegetative power
The weary eye may ken.'

But this is distinctly the impression of a first survey of the wild scene, though under glints of sunshine there will not fail to meet the eye little snatches of grassy bottom and stunted herbage, here and there in the midst of the rocks. Yet there is so little to relieve the singular darkness of the rock-pent water, and the dusky green of the Cuchullin hills that surround it, that one fully appreciates, even in the brightest weather, how true a picture Scott has drawn of the scene :—

'For rarely human eye has known
A scene so stern as that dread lake
With its dark ledge of barren stone.
Seems that primeval earthquake's sway
Hath rent a strange and shattered way
Through the rude bosom of the hill.
And that each naked precipice
Sable ravine and dark abyss
Tells of the outrage still.'

To see Coruisk in fine weather is impressive, but it is when leaden clouds weigh down the atmosphere, and dank mists clothe the rugged peaks around, that the scene comes out in its full and weird im-

G

pressiveness. Then 'naked precipice,' 'sable ravine,' and 'dark abyss,' are seen to be true words, and there comes on the spectator some feeling of scenes that have been read of in Dante or Milton:—

> 'He views
> The dismal situation, waste and wild.
> A dungeon horrible on all sides round * *
> Regions of sorrow, doleful shades, where peace
> And rest can never dwell.'

But we must not give too black a character to this loch and its surrounding hills. It is no Malebolge, filled by 'sounds and sights unholy,' and while it impresses by its solitude and grandeur, it also gratifies by its intense feeling of repose, and its remoteness from the ills of busier life. Those visiting Coruisk will view with wonder the extraordinary peaks of the Cuchullins, (pronounced Coolins,) each more fantastic and broken than his neighbour, and all consisting of the green-black hypersthene trap that gives its character to the scenery here. South-east of the loch is the mighty bulk of Blabheinn, (pronounced Blaven,) a huge mass with precipitous sides, down which, on the occurrence of one of the frequent showers of this watery isle, the rain is seen to descend in broken rills of dazzling whiteness, making an extraordinary effect upon the upright face of dark rock. To the north-east, the Cuchullin hills terminate in the ragged triple peak of Scuir-na-gillean, the rock or hill of the young men. This height was first scaled, in recorded history, in 1836, when Principal Forbes, of glacial fame, ascended it, and since then, with guides, it has been frequently climbed. But from the extraordinary formation of the hill, the ascent is a work of much danger, and lives have been lost in the attempt. The peak is a narrow ledge, precipitous on every side. The height is 3220 feet, and although Scuir-na-Banachtich, the westmost peak, is believed to be as high, it has not been climbed so far as is known, and thus Scuir-na-gillean holds first rank in this wonderful group of mountains.

LOCH MAREE.

THE first sight of this glorious loch, as the stage coach from Auchnasheen station brings the traveller to the top of a steep descent, is calculated to excite the liveliest emotions of wonder and surprise. The road reminds one of some Alpine pass, while far below stretches the large sheet of water, with its western end eighteen miles away. If for a moment a feeling of the smallness of the loch should supervene, the huge hills dwindling it down by their enormous bulk, this soon passes away, and we feel to be in presence of one of Scotland's proudest lochs. The coach drive to Gairloch occupies six hours in all, including a short stoppage to bait the horses at Kinlochewe, and during the whole time the eye is filled with pictures of grandeur or of delight. After the tedious descent to the water's edge has convinced you that the feeling of smallness is a mistake, you have time to observe the effect which such a mountain as Ben Slioch has in dwarfing all around it. Loch Maree is but six miles from the sea, with no great descent, so that the hill raises its mighty shoulders almost sheer from the sea level. From the road you perceive, skirting the loch on the other side, what seems a fringe of very small bushes. But anon a two-storey house appears among the bushes, which now, with a known standard of comparison, are seen to be tall trees! From the top of Ben Slioch, or any of the neighbouring mountains of first-class size, the view is grand, embracing at once the Atlantic and the German Oceans. On the opposite side from Ben Slioch is the Scottish *Pentelicus*, Ben Eay, whose brilliant white quartz pinnacle may sometimes be seen shining in the sun, like the famed marble mountains of Greece. On the bosom of Loch Maree, near its widest end, are several islands, the largest of which, Eilan Mhaolrubh, contains the remains of an old chapel, and a holy well that is even yet in high repute amongst the ignorant. It is sometimes said that the chapel, island, and loch get their name from the Virgin Mary, but this is now universally acknowledged amongst scholars to be an error. It was the Irish preacher, Maelrubha, (Latinised to Malrubius, then softened down in local tongues to Mulray, Mourie, and Maree,) who came over to Scotland in the seventh century, who gave his name to the place. Dr. Arthur Mitchell, in his Rhind Lectures on Civilization, has told in full the story of the curious superstitions concerning this island, of which examples as recently as twenty years ago are quoted. It is to be noted that when, a year or two ago, the Queen visited the island, great indignation was expressed in some quarters, because it was on a Sunday evening she got rowed over from her retreat at Talladale to see this interesting place.

The coach leaves the edge of the loch at Talladale, after a lovely and varied drive along its banks, now in the bosom of a dense wood, now in the midst of a rocky chaos,

'The fragments of an earlier world.'

A few miles down the road are found the romantic falls of the Kerry. The man on the box seat at the left of the coach looks sheer down the precipice over which the stream falls, as the coach with a swing turns the corner of the steep road, with little visible between the traveller and the dangers of that awful chasm!

THE CATARACT.

FALLS OF THE GARRAVALT.

ALTHOUGH not reckoning amongst the grander waterfalls of Scotland, the cataract on the Garravalt, in the Queen's Forest of Ballochbuie, is behind few in the picturesque wildness of its surroundings. The name in Gaelic,—'Garbh-allt'—is characteristic and descriptive, signifying a rough brook, and our view of the roaring cataract shews how completely it deserves that name. The entire course of the stream, from its rise in Cairn Taggart, one of the Loch-na-gar group of hills, is about five miles, and the linn itself is little more than half a mile from where the Garravalt joins the Dee. To reach the place,—and few visitors to the famed district of Deeside will omit to visit it,—only a slight deviation from the road leading from Crathie and Balmoral to the Castleton of Braemar is called for, the place where the road leads off being close beside the Bridge of Invercauld, over the Dee.

This waterfall, the finest of several in Deeside, has been enthusiastically praised by every writer. The Queen, in the *Leaves from the Journal of Our Life in the Highlands*, says, 'From the road in the wood we walked up to the *Falls of the Garbhall*, which are beautiful. The rocks are very grand, and the view from the little bridge, and also from a seat a little lower down, is very pretty.' Her Majesty has here indicated the two points of view generally chosen, namely that from the bridge looking down, and that from below, looking up the stream, the latter being adopted for our representation. To say, as one writer has done, that 'the water comes foaming and raging and toiling down in a manner almost impossible to be described,' is to abdicate the chief functions of a word painter. The waters come roaring and rushing down the rocky cleft, hurrying over the blocks and stones that impede their passage, and creating a noise that is heard far off,

> 'Confounding,
> Astounding,
> Dizzying and deafening the ear with its sound
> And so never ending, but always descending
> Sound and motion for ever and ever are blending.'

The eye never tires in looking at the lively scene, and the ear drinks in the murmuring and thundering sound, which has the usual faculty of swelling and falling, till the mind gets imbued with the idea that the waters are endowed with the faculty of speech, so that we involuntarily ask 'what are the wild waves saying?' and linger long at the spot in the vain hope that the varying syllables of the living water will yet form themselves into intelligible words. This is not to be however, and we may turn away to look for a moment at the picturesque country in which this attractive waterfall is situated. The steep pine-covered hill is called the Forest of Ballochbuie. Here again we may turn to the Queen's book, where 'the aspect of the wood which is called Balloch Buie' is described as 'most lovely.' It is said that this ground was at one time given to the Farquharsons of Invercauld, by the Earl of Mar, for a tartan plaid. It is now royal property, and forms an extensive and valued addition to the forest of Balmoral, which lies between Ballochbuie and the castle. It was in the Mar territory, at the Castleton of Braemar, that in 1715 the then Earl of Mar raised his standard in support of the Chevalier St. George, whom he had previously, in Glenlivat, proclaimed as King James the Eighth of Scotland. Here, where 'the gathering pipe on Loch-na-gar' was heard sounding 'long and sairly,' the inheritor of the crown of the Stewarts has frequently attended a very different gathering on the 'Braes o' Mar,' when the Duffs, the Farquharsons, and other clans meet, not for feuds and bloodshed, but for the athletic rivalries of 'tossing the caber' and other native games.

THE DHU LOCH—LOCH-NA-GAR.

IT is perhaps puzzling to the stranger to learn that Loch-na-gar is a mountain, 3768 feet above the level of the sea, though there is on the summit, and hemmed in by steep precipices, a small sheet of water that gives its name to the hill. But in the Dhu Loch, a little further in the heart of this mountainous district, we find one of the most striking scenes in Scotland. It was of the hill and its surroundings that Lord Byron wrote his familiar lines,

> "Away ye gay landscapes, ye gardens of roses,
> In you let the minions of luxury rove.
> Restore me the rocks where the snowflake reposes,
> Tho' still they are sacred to freedom and love.
> O Caledonia, beloved are thy mountains,
> Round their white summits though elements war,
> Though cataracts foam, 'stead of smooth-flowing fountains,
> I sigh for the valley of dark Loch-na-gar.

The *Dhu Loch*, or black loch—a well-deserved name—has its bed, as shown in our view, in steep and desperate precipices of granite, and for sternness of outline is not excelled. The red-deer on its banks are undisturbed, for seldom does the foot of man intrude on their repose, and while the water is clear, it is strongly discoloured by the peat, and the absence of foliage, with the sterile loneliness of the scene, make men shun rather than court its remote solitudes. 'The scenery is beautiful here,' says the Queen, in her *Leaves from the Journal of our Life in the Highlands*, 'so wild and grand,—real severe Highland scenery,' and the description is surely a true one. No one can come about the Dhu Loch without being prepared for 'several scrambles,' like the royal party, and without being prepared also to endure the 'severity' as well as enjoy the beauty of the place. If he does not, like Lord Byron, admit Loch-na-gar to be 'the most sublime and picturesque of Caledonian Alps,' —for perhaps some hill already named in this volume, unknown to Byron, such as Blaven, or Ben Eay, might dispute the title—still he will acknowledge that it is a wonderful region. It is said that on a fair calculation of what elements go to make up a desirable climate, the kingdom has nothing better to offer than Braemar, and that Balmoral is the ideal site for a residence. The district is like all that belonged to the little bear in the child's story. The hills are neither too high nor too low, but just right. The climate is neither too mild nor too severe, but just right. The rainfall is neither too much nor too little, but just right. In short it is a perfect region,—perfect in its variety of scenery, from the rich wood-lands of its lower ranges to the wild grandeur of its mountain recesses. Perfect is it also in its fine lochs, its picturesque waterfalls, its brattling burns, and its rolling rivers.

The waters from the Dhu Loch run into Loch Muick, above which lies the hut at Altnaghuissac, a favourite *shiel*, or mountain summer house of the royal family when living at Balmoral. This lies in the very innermost recesses of a grand region, and here the pure air, and the splendid views, combine to make a haven of re-treat, whether, as in the case of royalty, from the cares of state and the turmoil of politics, or, in the case of the jaded man of business, from the burdens and anxieties of the daily grind of life. Those characteristics, more or less true of the whole inner region of Aberdeenshire, have made the district a favourite *sanitarium*, while for the mere pleasure-seeker it presents a succession of delights, full of unalloyed beauty, unless indeed the weather should break down, and the unwary traveller is caught in the rains and mists of winter, which may make the ascent of Loch-na-gar dangerous.

THE CAULDRON LINN.

(*View on Title-page.*)

IT is not a little remarkable that the only conception of the Devon put on paper by Robert Burns was as a clear winding river, whose sweet stream 'meandering flows.' The fact was that Burns was led to know that something was expected of him, and his muse was not to respond, for she acted spontaneously or not at all. A woman did eventually inspire him to write—ah! those women, how much of Burns' best thoughts did they command!—and he referred to the romantic stream only in order to tell that the 'bonniest flower' there had once been a sweet bud on the banks of his own beloved Ayr. The river Devon has a short and chequered existence, and after a course of thirty-four miles, falls into the Forth within five miles of its source. At that little bit of its journey when, after rising in Stirlingshire, it flows through Perthshire into Kinrosshire, and then doubles back across a peninsular bit of Perthshire to reach the county of Clackmannan, the stream goes through a series of vicissitudes that completely destroy its 'clear-winding' character. First there is the deep chasm across which the Rumbling Bridge is thrown. There are here two bridges, one over the other. The earlier bridge, built in 1713, eighty feet above the stream, is narrow and without a parapet, and there is a local tradition of a man who fell asleep in his cart being taken home safely over this exalted and narrow pathway by the instinct of his horse. The present bridge, a plain but strong erection, was built in 1816, and is one hundred and twenty feet above the stream, the latter hidden far below amidst inaccessible precipices and darkening woods. Further up the stream is the 'Devil's Mill,' said to be a waterfall, but so completely inaccessible, that the character of the place is very much a matter of conjecture. However, there is heard far down in the depths below the clack and beat of a mill; and as this goes on Sabbath and Saturday alike, the name quoted above has been bestowed on the unhallowed mill. It is understood that the water falls into a basin or chasm without outlet, carrying air with it, then the air bursts out with the boom that resembles the regulated beat of a mill. Be the cause what it may, the delusion is perfect.

Pursuing its way for a mile through a deeply cleft and gnarled valley, the Devon flings itself in desperation over the Cauldron Linn. There are two points of view for this singular waterfall, one from above looking down, the other, shown in our view, from below, looking up. From above, at the level where the trees are seen, the water leaps into the cauldrons that give the Linn its name. In the hard basaltic rock the swirling water has worn out three circular vats or cauldrons, in which the stream incessantly goes round. The surplus water plunges over the edge of one cauldron to that below, or, as in one instance, has worn a hole in the side of the pot, and rushes through that. It is said that when a sheep's carcase is brought down, and the river is not high, it will swirl round in the cauldrons till a spate comes strong enough to carry it over the edge. At the top the round lips of the upper cauldron nearly meet, so that a man of nerve could leap across. The distance is probably not over a yard, but so dizzying is the incessant whirl of the water, that so far from leaping across, a timid visitor may not even look over the edge, unless prone on the earth he puts his face over, conscious that six-sevenths of his body are safe on *terra firma!*

From below none of this terrible stir of the Cauldron Linn is seen—we have merely a snowy sheet of water, beautiful certainly, and impressive in its height, and encircled with lofty precipices, so that, without reference to its characteristic features above, it takes rank as one of the most beautiful cataracts in Scotland. The view, which forms a vignette on our title-page, would in its natural place come before or after Loch Leven.

H. FAWCETT, ENGRAVER AND PRINTER, DRIFFIELD.

www.ingramcontent.com/pod-product-compliance
Lightning Source LLC
Chambersburg PA
CBHW031439280326
41927CB00038B/987